# COPING WITH . . .
# GLASS
# TRASH

▼ ▼ ▼ ▼ ▼ ▼ ▼ ▼ ▼ ▼ ▼ ▼ ▼ ▼ ▼ ▼

# COPING WITH . . .
# GLASS
# TRASH

Jamie Daniel • Veronica Bonar
Illustrated by Tony Kenyon

Gareth Stevens Publishing
**MILWAUKEE**

**For a free color catalog describing Gareth Stevens' list of high-quality books, call 1-800-341-3569 (USA) or 1-800-461-9120 (Canada).**

**Library of Congress Cataloging-in-Publication Data**

Daniel, Jamie.
    Coping with— glass trash/adapted from Veronica Bonar's Glass rubbish! by Jamie
Daniel; illustrated by Tony Kenyon. — North American ed.
       p. cm. — (Trash busters)
    Includes bibliographical references and index.
    ISBN 0-8368-1057-0
    1. Glass waste—Juvenile literature.  2. Refuse and refuse disposal—Juvenile literature.
[1. Glass—Recycling.  2. Refuse and refuse disposal.  3. Recycling (Waste)]  I. Kenyon,
Tony, ill.  II. Bonar, Veronica. Glass rubbish!  III. Title.  IV. Series: Daniel, Jamie.
Trash busters.
TD799.D36   1994                                   93-32483

This North American edition first published in 1994 by

**Gareth Stevens Publishing**
1555 North RiverCenter Drive, Suite 201
Milwaukee, WI 53212, USA

Series editor: Patricia Lantier-Sampon
Cover design: Karen Knutson

**Picture Credits:**
The Environmental Picture Library p. 13 (Charlotte MacPherson); Robert Harding Picture Library pp. 8, 21; Courtesy of the Museum of London p. 24; Oxford Scientific Films p. 14 (Mike Birkhead), p. 17 (Steffen Hauser); Science Photo Library p. 19 (Heini Schneebeli); Zefa pp. 7, 11, 26.

Printed in the USA

1 2 3 4 5 6 7 8 9 99 98 97 96 95 94

At this time, Gareth Stevens, Inc., does not use 100 percent recycled paper, although the paper used in our books does contain about 30 percent recycled fiber. This decision was made after a careful study of current recycling procedures revealed their dubious environmental benefits. We will continue to explore recycling options.

# TABLE OF CONTENTS

Words that appear in the glossary are printed in **boldface** type the first time they occur in the text.

# WHY GLASS IS USEFUL

Glass is a sturdy material that does not rust or wear out. It can be formed into many shapes. It is also **transparent**, which means light can pass through it.

Many items we use every day are made of glass. There are glass bottles, mirrors, windows, television screens, light bulbs, and **thermometers**. Thermometers are used to measure our body temperature.

6

We buy items such as jam, pickles, juice, and hot sauce in glass bottles and jars. Glass containers do not scratch or melt as easily as plastic containers.

Some people just throw away empty glass containers. But most people realize that these containers can be washed and reused or recycled.

➤ Glass bottles and jars often break when they are thrown away.

7

# HOW GLASS IS MADE

The first people to make glass were the ancient Egyptians. They discovered that heating sand and ash together produced a strong, transparent material. This material was also soft and easy to shape when heated at high temperatures.

➡ This wall painting shows ancient Egyptians drinking from glass cups.

We use the same **raw materials** to make glass today. Most glass is a combination of sand, **soda ash**, and **limestone**.

These materials are heated in a **furnace** to a temperature of between 2,372°F (1,300°C) and 2,732°F (1,500°C). The mixture changes into **molten** glass, which can then be easily shaped.

Skilled glassblowers make molten glass into beautiful and useful items. Factory-made glass is formed into shapes using **molds**. Window glass is made by flattening molten glass with big rollers.

If a thread is pulled through molten glass, a thin glass tube will form around it. Some thermometer tubes are made this way.

10

Glass can be made into tiny **fibers** as thin as a human hair. These fibers can be used as **insulation** material to keep heat from escaping from buildings.

When glass fibers are combined with plastic, they make a light, strong material called **fiberglass**. Among other things, fiberglass is used to make fishing rods, suitcases, and car bodies.

▲ Glass fibers carry light from one place to another.

# BROKEN GLASS

Glass can shatter into many splinters, called **shards**. Even tiny shards of glass are dangerous and can easily pierce human and animal skin. If you accidentally break any glass, ask a grown-up to come right away to help you.

↟ Broken glass on the beach is hard to see and easy to step on.

Small pieces of broken glass should be swept or vacuumed. Large pieces can be carefully picked up by a grown-up. But all broken glass should be carefully wrapped before placing it in the trash can. Trash collectors do not want to get cut, either!

# GLASS LITTER

Broken glass left on a beach or elsewhere is dangerous. People and animals can get badly hurt if they walk on the glass and cut their feet.

Animals can also be killed by discarded glass containers. They crawl inside the containers to search for food and cannot get out again. These animals then starve to death.

⬆ This fox could cut itself on shards of glass.

Glass **litter** can also cause fires. When the sun's rays shine through glass, they heat up dry grass or leaves underneath. The grass and leaves may catch fire. Large areas of countryside and forests can be destroyed by fires like this.

# GLASS TRASH

Some people think the best way to get rid of glass is to break it into pieces and bury it in the ground. But buried glass does not break down like dead plants or animals. It can stay exactly the same even when buried for hundreds of years.

Other people throw glass into their trash. But bottles, jars, and other glass containers take up a lot of space in **landfills** where trash is buried. Then new landfill sites must be found. This destroys a lot of the countryside.

⬆ Glass piles up fast at landfills.

# WASTING GLASS
# AND FUEL

Glass is one of the heaviest materials in our trash. In general, garbage trucks use a lot of fuel collecting all our trash and carrying it to landfills. But they must use even more fuel when there is a lot of glass in the trash because glass is so heavy.

The raw materials used to make glass are inexpensive. However, it takes a lot of **energy** to dig out the sand, and more fuel to transport the raw materials to the factories that make glass. Even more energy is used to heat the furnaces where glass is melted and shaped.

▲ The glass in this furnace is so hot it glows white and yellow.

# RECYCLING GLASS

People use billions of glass bottles and jars every year. But, fortunately, many of these glass containers do not end up in landfills. People who care about the environment place their glass containers in pick-up bins or take their glass to a **recycling center**. These centers collect glass, separated by color, for **recycling**.

▲ Glass bottles are sorted by color during the recycling process.

The collected glass is taken to glass factories. There, it is placed into furnaces, along with new molten glass for added quality. The recycled glass melts fast, so it takes less energy to turn it into new glass than to make new glass from raw materials only.

# RECYCLING RULES

It is important to sort glass containers and bottles for recycling by color into clear, brown, and green glass. Even small amounts of brown glass mixed in with clear glass can change the color of a new container that might be made from the recycled glass.

Before taking glass to a recycling center, be sure it is clean and remove any metal or plastic parts. These materials weaken new glass made from recycled glass.

Some glass items, such as window panes, light bulbs, and mirrors, cannot be recycled easily. The raw materials used to make these items are different from other glass items. These objects should be placed in a separate container for recycling.

# BOTTLES WITH LONG LIVES

At one time, bottles were all made by hand, so they were very expensive. People did not throw them away after one use, but used them again and again.

Some bottles made today are also made to last a long time. These are called **returnable bottles**. They are made of tough glass that does not break easily.

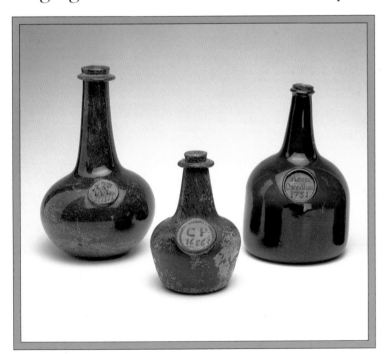

↞ People used to put seals on their bottles to show who owned them.

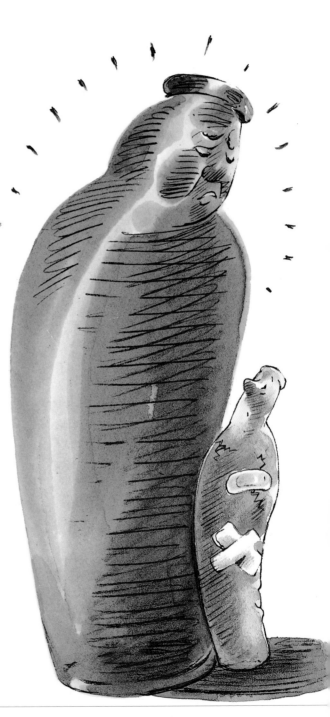

Returnable bottles are usually use drinks. They must be **sterilized** cleaned in boiling water, before they can be refilled. In some places, people must pay a small extra fee, called a **deposit**, when they buy returnable bottles. They get the money back when they return the bottles.

# REUSING GLASS

▲ Used glass jars can be very handy for storing food and household items.

Empty glass containers can be reused in many ways. Some people use juice bottles over again to make their own juice or iced tea. Jam and peanut butter jars are sometimes designed to be reused as drinking glasses. Look for containers like these the next time you visit the grocery store.

Empty bottles and jars are useful in other ways. For example, tall jars can be used as flower vases. A very big jar can be used as a goldfish bowl. And placing a glass jar over a small seedling for a while will help it grow. The jar collects and keeps moisture and acts as a miniature **greenhouse** for the plant!

Recycling glass and reusing glass containers is easy, practical, and helpful to the environment.

# GLOSSARY

**deposit:** a small amount of extra money paid at the time of purchase. People usually pay deposits on returnable bottles. They get the money back if and when they return the bottles.

**energy:** the power necessary to do any sort of work. We eat food to get the energy we need for our bodies, and machines make energy from different types of fuel.

**fiberglass:** a light, strong material made of glass strands, or fibers, that are mixed with plastic.

**fibers:** thin strands of an artificial or natural substance.

**furnace:** a big, enclosed space like an oven in which a high-temperature fire can burn. Furnaces are often used to melt metals or glass.

**greenhouse:** a room or building, usually made of glass, where plants that need warm, moist temperatures can grow.

**insulation:** materials used to line or cover other materials, such as the building materials used in houses to prevent heat, electricity, or sound from escaping. Fiberglass is a good insulating material.

**landfills:** big holes in the ground where trash is dumped and then covered with soil.

**limestone:** a type of rock used in making glass. Limestone is also used in construction and to make cement.

**litter:** the trash people carelessly throw on the ground and in other places.

**molds:** hollow shapes into which substances are placed while they are still soft from being heated.

**molten:** softer and more liquid than the original state as a result of being heated.

**raw materials:** the basic natural ingredients, or materials, from which something is made.

**recycling:** the process of making a new product from old products that have already been used. Many metal, glass, plastic, wood, and paper products can be recycled.

**recycling center:** a place where materials are gathered to be recycled, or prepared for reuse.

**returnable bottles:** bottles that can be brought back to the place of purchase so they can be recycled.

**shards:** pieces of broken glass. Shards of glass can cause deep, dangerous cuts.

**soda ash:** a material produced when a metal called sodium is burned. Soda ash is used in making glass.

**sterilize:** to make objects germ-free. Bottles can be sterilized by boiling them in water.

**thermometers:** thin glass tubes filled with mercury, used for measuring temperatures.

**transparent:** allowing light to pass through, so that objects on the other side of it are visible. Glass is often transparent.

# PLACES TO WRITE AND VISIT

Here are some places you can write or visit for more information about glass and recycling. If you write, be sure to give your name and address and be clear about what you would like to know. Include a stamped, self-addressed envelope for a reply.

The National Recycling
   Coalition
1101 30th Street NW
Suite 305
Washington, D.C. 20007

The Museum of Science
   and Industry
1000 Soldier Field
Chicago, IL 60605

Greenpeace Foundation
185 Spadina Avenue
Sixth Floor
Toronto, Ontario
M5T 2C6

# INTERESTING FACTS ABOUT GLASS

**Did you know . . .**

- that fiberglass is used to make all kinds of things you might not expect to be made from glass, such as drapes, upholstery material, and artificial arms and legs?

- that what we call "glasses" — eyeglasses that help people see better — are often not made of glass at all? Many "glasses" are now made of plastic because it makes eyeglasses lighter and more comfortable than glass.

- that glass mirrors can be made that are mirrors on one side, but transparent on the other? People on the transparent side can see those on the other, but people on the mirror side see only themselves in the glass!

# MORE BOOKS TO READ

*From Sand to Glass.*  Ali Mitgutsch  (Carolrhoda)

*Garbage and Recycling.*  Judith Woodburn (Gareth Stevens)

*Glass.*  Jane Chandler (Garrett Educational Corporation)

*Kid Heroes of the Environment.  Simple Things Kids are Doing to Save the Earth.*  EarthWorks Group Staff (EarthWorks)

*Reducing, Reusing, and Recycling.*  Bobby Kalman (Crabtree)

*What We Can Do About Recycling Garbage.*  Donna Bailey (Watts)

*Why Does Litter Cause Problems?*  Isaac Asimov (Gareth Stevens)

# INDEX